The Long Journey of Central Bank Communication

The Long Journey of Central Bank Communication

Otmar Issing

The MIT Press
Cambridge, Massachusetts
London, England

This book was set in Palatino by Westchester Publishing Services. Printed and bound in the United States of America.

Library of Congress Cataloging-in-Publication Data

Names: Issing, Otmar, author.
Title: The long journey of central bank communication / Otmar Issing.
Description: Cambridge, MA : MIT Press, [2019] | Series: Karl Brunner distinguished lecture series | Includes bibliographical references and index.
Identifiers: LCCN 2019005730 | ISBN 9780262537858 (pbk. : alk. paper)
Subjects: LCSH: Banks and banking, Central. | Communication in financial institutions.
Classification: LCC HG1811 .I87 2019 | DDC 332.1/1--dc23
LC record available at https://lccn.loc.gov/2019005730

10 9 8 7 6 5 4 3 2 1

Contents

Series Foreword

The Swiss National Bank is grateful to Otmar Issing for writing this book, in which he revisits and develops the ideas presented in his Karl Brunner Distinguished Lecture of September 20, 2018. The series of books associated with the Karl Brunner Distinguished Lecture explores topics of key importance to central banking.

The Karl Brunner Distinguished Lecture Series, which is organized by the Swiss National Bank and takes place annually in Zurich, honors eminent monetary theory and policy thinkers whose research has influenced central banking. The scope of the lecture reflects the attention Karl Brunner devoted to monetary economics, his belief in the need to advance theoretical and applied analysis in this field, and, in particular, his concern for the policy relevance of economic science.

Thomas J. Jordan, Chairman of the Governing Board

Preface

This book is a substantial expansion of the Karl Brunner Distinguished Lecture I gave at the invitation of the Swiss National Bank on September 20, 2018, in Zurich, Switzerland. In effect, it is really the other way around: I first wrote this text, from which I presented an excerpt in my lecture. I have since continued to work on the manuscript.

Over time, I have received valuable comments from Klaus Adam, Charles Goodhart, Michael Ehrmann, Benjamin Friedman, Mervyn King, Emmanuel Mönch, Elke Muchlinski, Jan Frederik Qvigstad, Helmut Siekmann, Bernhard Winkler, and Uwe Walz. Three anonymous reviewers have sent very constructive suggestions. Finally, the editorial team at the MIT Press has done an excellent job. To all of them I am enormously grateful.

This book tries to cover the main strands of the literature. At the same time, I could not have written it without having experience as a central banker—two periods of eight years each, first at the Deutsche Bundesbank and thereafter at the European Central Bank. At both central banks I had key responsibilities for monetary policy, including the corresponding communication. During these sixteen years I enjoyed being in contact with many colleagues from the world of central banking as well as with academics, which gave me many opportunities to discuss issues relevant to the topic.

The book is organized as follows. After a short introduction, chapter 2 briefly explains the development from secretiveness to transparency by central banks. Chapter 3 clarifies some terminological issues, and chapter 4 describes the relationship between practice and theory of communication. Chapter 5 is devoted to the challenge for central bank communication to increase the effectiveness of monetary policy. Guiding expectations is the main task, with forward guidance as a new element in the context of the zero lower bound. Decision-making on monetary policy by committees causes specific problems for communication. The last paragraph analyzes the relationship between communication and financial markets as its foremost addressee. Accountability and transparency are identified in chapters 6 and 7 as crucial challenges for central bank communication. Chapter 8 highlights the main results.

Otmar Issing
Center for Financial Studies,
Goethe University Frankfurt

1 Introduction

It is a privilege to give this lecture, which is devoted to the memory of Karl Brunner. His work—mostly in cooperation with the late Allan Meltzer—had a great influence on the discussion of the monetary transmission process and the importance and limits of monetary policy. His seminal contributions are well known, but I will note that those engaged in monetary theory would be well advised to give new attention to the role of relative prices and portfolio considerations, which are missing from highly sophisticated but at the same time simplistic models. It is striking that this groundbreaking research, which includes the work of James Tobin, is widely ignored. (In a 2018 survey by Eusepi and Preston, "The Science of Monetary Policy: An Imperfect Knowledge Perspective," these names, along with that of Milton Friedman, are missing.) Referring to the root of the 2008 financial crisis, Benjamin Friedman, in his contribution to the "Swiss National Bank Karl Brunner Centenary"

(Friedman 2016, 5) remarked: "If the instincts of more macroeconomists had been channeled along the lines laid out in any of the early Brunner-Meltzer models ... not only might these dangerous developments have attracted attention earlier but the implications for economic policy might have been better understood."

Under the leadership of its chairman, Thomas Jordan, the Swiss National Central Bank has strengthened its research links. The establishment of the annual Karl Brunner Distinguished Lecture Series honors an outstanding scholar of monetary theory and demonstrates the bank's affinity with the domain of research. It is a privilege to have been invited to give this lecture, in a series that started with two academics of the highest repute, namely, Kenneth Rogoff and John Taylor.

I met Karl Brunner at the Konstanz Seminars and had stimulating discussions with him on the occasion of a lecture he gave at my invitation at my home University of Würzburg. In a long bilateral meeting, he insisted on rigorous analysis and clear argumentation.

His respect for central bankers was, however, extremely limited, to say the least. At that time I had not the slightest idea that years later I would become a member of this group.

Here is his devastating statement:

Central Banking [has been] traditionally surrounded by a peculiar and protective political mystique. The political mystique of Central Banking was, and still is to some extent, widely expressed by an essentially metaphysical approach to monetary affairs and monetary policy-making.... The mystique thrives on a pervasive impression that Central Banking is an esoteric art. Access to this art and its proper execution is confined to the initiated elite. The esoteric nature of the art is moreover revealed by an inherent impossibility to articulate its insights in explicit and intelligible words and sentences. Communication with the uninitiated breaks down. (Brunner 1981)

2　From Ignorance to Triumph

2.1　Once upon a Time

Brunner's verdict, which might sound like a caricature of central bankers, has been topped by reality in the past. Probably the most famous case was delivered by the Bank of England in the 1930s. At that time the bank was seen as the epitome of reticence vis-à-vis the public and was subject to increasing criticism (King 2004). As a consequence, the Committee on Finance and Industry, also known as the Macmillan Committee, visited the bank. Deputy Governor Sir Ernest Harvey defended the bank's position (Macmillan 1931, 27–31):

Committee member Gregory:　I should like to ask you, Sir Ernest, whether you have ever considered the possibility of the Bank issuing an Annual Report on the lines of the Annual Report of the Federal Reserve Board, for instance?

Deputy Governor Harvey:　I confess I am sometimes nervous at the thought of publication unless it is historical. The question is whether, when it is merely historical it is of any particular value, or whether from the fact that it is issued from the central bank undue importance may be attributed to certain things that are stated, more importance than perhaps they merit....

Committee member Keynes: Arising from Professor Gregory's questions, is it a practice of the Bank of England never to explain what your policy is?

Harvey: Well, I think it has been our practice to leave our actions to explain our policy.

Keynes: Or the reasons for its policy?

Harvey: It is a dangerous thing to start to give reasons.

Keynes: Or to defend itself against criticism?

Harvey: As regards criticism, I am afraid, though the Committee may not all agree, we do not admit there is need for defence; to defend ourselves is somewhat akin to a lady starting to defend her virtue.

2.2   Times Have Changed

To paraphrase a Roman proverb, times are changing, and central banks are changing with them. This is nowhere more evident than in banks' moving from secretiveness to transparency. Active communication has become a favorite tool of most central banks.

The so far most effective example was delivered by Mario Draghi, president of the European Central Bank (ECB). On July 26, 2012, he made his magical statement: "Within our mandate, the ECB is ready to do whatever it

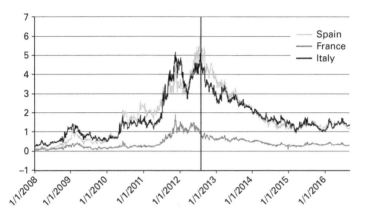

Figure 2.1
Ten-year government bond spreads in Spain, France, and Italy relative to Germany's (in percentage points). The bold vertical line denotes the day of Draghi's "whatever it takes" speech. *Source:* ECB.

takes to preserve the euro. And believe me, it will be enough" (Draghi 2012).

These words were followed by the announcement of the Outright Monetary Transactions (OMT) program. Immediately after Draghi's speech, the spreads of ten-year government bonds in Spain, France, and Italy relative to Germany's declined from their temporary peak to previous levels. Until today, not a single euro has been spent to intervene under this program. Words, communication alone, did the work. However, this effect cannot be separated from the person and the position of the originator (see Muchlinski 2014).

Impressive as this case is, the fact that announcements of actions that may lie in the near or more distant future may have an immediate effect can be observed many times in the course of history. A remarkable historical example dates back to Roman times (see Issing 1985). In 67 BC, when pirates in the Mediterranean Sea posed an ever-greater threat to the supply of grain, the Roman authorities assigned command of a huge naval force to Gnaeus Pompeius. Pompeius delivered on his command and rid the sea of pirates within forty days. A year later, in his first political speech, "De imperio Gnaei Pompeii," Marcus Tullius Cicero remarked that on the same day that Pompeius was assigned this command, the price of grain fell suddenly from its highest level, thanks to the hope placed in this man, to a level that could hardly have been achieved through a long period of peace and outstanding crop fertility (Cicero [ca. 66 BC] 1989).

This is an impressive historical example, and one can be sure there are numerous others, even in earlier times. Indeed, it is no coincidence that characterizations of communication strategies have started to refer to ancient Greece. "Delphic" and "Odyssean" communications are now followed by "Aesopian" forward guidance (Moessner, Jansen, and de Haan 2017). Whatever the usefulness of such headlines may be, Cicero leaves no doubt in his speech that the basis for effective communication is credibility. The "announcement effect" of the command for Pompeius was due to his reputation, based on his delivery on previous commitments.

This aspect will be discussed later in detail. However, with all the progress and sophistication of communication in general and by central banks in particular, the importance of credibility should never be neglected.

3 A Short Terminology

Central bank communication in general terms can be defined as any information provided by the central bank and its representatives to the public. This includes all fields in which the central bank has a responsibility or mandate. In this text, financial stability and supervision are excluded (see, e.g., Born, Ehrmann, and Fratzscher 2013). As a consequence, central bank communication is restricted to public statements related to monetary policy, which encompasses information on the objective of monetary policy, the monetary policy strategy, decisions made and the reasoning behind them, the economic outlook, and future policy decisions (see also Blinder et al. 2008).

The tools for conveying information have changed over time. In the past, movements of the governors' eyebrows or the size of Greenspan's famous briefcase were interpreted as signals of potential changes in monetary policy. This interest can be seen as a desire, a demand for the central bank to give some information at a time when it was restrictive in this regard. From the perspective of the central bank, it just cannot escape giving information, deliberately or not, even when remaining absolutely silent. "It is not possible to avoid communication" can be called the iron law of communication theory (Muchlinsky 2001, 224).

The time of smoke signals is long past. Today central banks use all means of communication, and many studies attempt to ascertain which tools are most effective. Unfortunately, television is hardly appropriate for central bank communication. Televised press conferences of public statements would normally be followed only by specific groups, such as bank economists and journalists. Should high central bank representatives participate in televised talk shows? Is the risk of getting into policy debates and giving misguiding messages not too high? And appropriate communication by means of social media is difficult. As a consequence, central banks are restricted in their ability to directly address the public at large and continue to rely on mediation by the media.

A more or less comprehensive list of communication tools is presented by Issing (2005; see table A.1 in the appendix to this work). Several studies try to assess the relative importance of different tools (e.g., Barclays 2013; Blinder et al. 2017).

The key goal of central bank communication is to make monetary policy more effective. The underlying philosophy or theory is that better-informed actors—that is, those better informed on the policy of the central bank— make better, that is, more effective, decisions. The focus is on guiding and anchoring expectations about future actions of the central bank.

There are two more dimensions of central bank communication. Over time the demand for transparency of public institutions has risen dramatically and in many democratic countries has become a legal obligation. A logically distinct but interrelated aspect is accountability, which tends to correlate with the independence of central banks.

This triad raises the question of whether central bank communication with the goal of enhancing the effectiveness of monetary policy is coherent with the need to satisfy transparency and accountability obligations. Or can conflicts among these three objectives of central bank communication arise?

4 Communication—Practice and Theory

The development of central bank communication has been an evolutionary process. Driven more by outside critics than by intrinsic motivation, central banks started with rather cautious acts of communication and triggered a development toward further steps that was hard to control. A telling example is offered by the Fed, which—though hard to believe today—for a long time did not even make its monetary policy decisions public. An exception is the case of the ECB, which, as the youngest central bank of our time started from scratch, had to adopt a modern communication strategy and set a precedent by introducing a regular press conference beginning with a live statement on the reasoning behind the decision just made.

Overall this was a process of learning by doing. Every step in this evolution was a kind of experiment, and central banks learned from the successes and failures of different communication tools. Or, to put it differently, for a long time central bank communication more or less ignored the theory of communication.

Claude Shannon's (1948) mathematical theory of communication demonstrated that publishing an almost unlimited amount of information may not ensure that this information reaches the recipient, as the recipient's ability to process information might be limited. This was well recognized in macro-monetary models (Sims 2003; Adam 2004).

Winkler (2000) highlighted the need for clarity and a "common understanding" between the sender and recipients of central bank communication with a reference to Wittgenstein (1922), who started with a strict position about the clarity of language and ended by accepting a multiplicity of meaning in the use of language. These are only a few aspects that may be relevant. However, these findings were more or less neglected in the practice of central bank communication. Qvigstad and Schei (2018) analyze empirically what represents clear language. Clarity is a key element, but additional requirements are logical explanation, language that can be understood by the respective audience, and efficient writing that concentrates on the key factors, with less relevant information stripped away. Their research concentrates on written justifications for decisions but can serve as a guidance for communication in general.

Experience has shown how difficult it is to give the public all information in a way that is not only exhaustive but also clear and comprehensible (see Issing 2005). Kahneman (2003) has revealed the limits of human information-processing skills in his psychological research.

The weighing of information greatly depends on its intuitive accessibility. In addition, information is generally simplified and categorized before it is collated. Agents might interpret the same news differently, and their different interpretations can change over time according to movements of optimism or pessimism. As a consequence, what the central bank as sender will see as objective information is exposed to the subjectivity of receivers (de Grauwe 2013). Under these circumstances, how can the central bank solve the problem of conveying the necessary information clearly and with the appropriate emphasis and salience?

One option is to concentrate information into so-called code words, which are intended to signal the central bank's assessment of its present and future monetary policy in the simplest possible way. In the course of 2000, for instance, the ECB signaled its concern about rising risks to price stability by communicating that the ECB council was "vigilant" toward inflation. Such a code word, on the one hand, gives a clear signal that the ECB would leave no doubt over its commitment to its objective of maintaining price stability. On the other hand, underlying inflationary pressure hardly remains constant over time, and the central bank's assessment of this risk would continuously change accordingly. The same code word, "vigilant," may thus simply reaffirm the unchanged commitment of the ECB to its mandate. However, it could also be interpreted as a gradual change in the assessment of the risks to price stability, signaling a forthcoming policy decision. Code words and coded language in general cannot be separated from the context—here, of inflationary pressure as assessed by the central bank—and may lead to undue simplification or a "shortcut" replacing a more complete communication of a full-fledged assessment. "The use of code words implies the danger of misunderstanding and of veiling the context in which a central bank has to operate flexibly and decisively. Contrary to its assumed beneficial effects, the use of coded language will create and exacerbate situations where parties are misled and misunderstood" (Muchlinsky 2011, 225).

In this vein, Friedrich von Hayek ([1962] 2007, 21) criticized communication theory for its belief in the ability to communicate without explaining content or the process of achieving understanding.

This risk must be taken all the more seriously when the markets and the media are inclined to interpret the central bank's communication by analyzing a number of code words. As an illustration of this problem, a German financial newspaper, the *Börsen-Zeitung*, on August 9, 2003, published a whole lexicography of the ECB's codes as they were perceived by the media. The glossary is in German and was developed and extended over time. In his press conference of early October 2002, ECB president Willem F. Duisenberg told a journalist that he should make use of the "explanatory bible" published in the *Börsen-Zeitung* to interpret correctly his remarks on the future interest rate policy of the ECB.

A more recent example is provided in the Introductory Statement of April 26, 2016, by President Mario Draghi: "In the end, steady hand were words used in the discussion in the Governing Council.... Therefore the other words we used were patience, prudence first of all in assessing patience and persistence. Finally, it goes without saying that the Governing Council shares its steadfast commitment to price stability."

The focus of this communication is typically on financial markets, on its actors and observers. Central banks, however, have a much wider audience (see the appendix to this book). It is obvious that communication with academics needs a totally different approach than communication with the broader public. Both, in turn, differ from the information-processing mode and very short-term horizons applied by traders in the financial markets. Central bank communication has to cover a wide spectrum and has to master the great challenge of making all messages consistent, that is, of avoiding any potential misunderstandings that could easily arise if recipients belonging to one group—say, academics—were also following publications addressed to other audiences.

While professionals closely follow the central bank's communication, its impact on households (and firms) seems to be rather limited. Even when an initial effect can be identified, it tends to disappear within six months. Coibion and coworkers (2018) suggest that central banks should try to address this audience directly with more accessible messages and using the broad spectrum of new media. It remains to be seen whether central banks will follow this line and to what extent this will be successful. Would the credibility and reputation of central banks ultimately suffer from entering, for example, the realm of Twitter?

Another approach has been taken by the new governor of the Reserve Bank of New Zealand, Adrian Orr, who presented his monetary policy statement by making jokes and using colorful illustrations in order to "demystify monetary policy," as reporters for Reuters put it (Greenfield and Wardell 2018). It remains to be seen whether this kind of presentation will broaden the coverage and continue to satisfy the expectations of professionals. And can we be sure that the credibility and reputation of a central bank will not suffer from the governor making jokes on such occasions?

Incidentally, I am reminded of a rather odd episode. When I was responsible for preparing the introductory statement to the ECB press conference by the president, I was asked by some members of the Governing Council to bring new words into the otherwise boring text. I warned that such a change of words—with the intention of an otherwise unchanged message—might create confusion. Finally, I accepted, partly to demonstrate the counterproductiveness of such a ploy. I replaced "vigilant" with "alert," after having clarified with language experts that these words were synonymous. The council approved the text with the new term "alert," and the result was as I had expected. Some media reported that the council was no longer "vigilant" but "only alert" (see Issing 2000).

Günter Coenen and coworkers (2017) have explored how the major communication tools of the ECB and the Fed have evolved over time concerning readability and length. In figure 4.1, readability is represented by the Flesh-Kinkaid reading-grade-level statistic, which measures the years of formal education that are required to under-

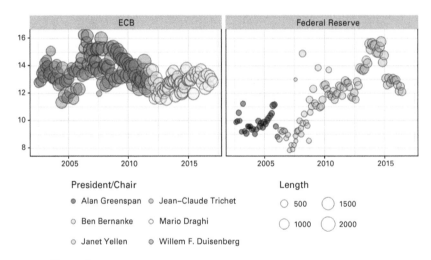

Figure 4.1
Length of ECB/FOMC monetary policy statements and difficulty of language employed, by president or chair. *Source:* Günter Coenen et al., "Communication of Monetary Policy in Unconventional Times," ECB Working Paper 2080 (Frankfurt am Main: European Central Bank, June 2017), 10.

stand the message. Length is measured by the number of words through the size of the cycle. The figure compares the introductory statements by the president of the ECB and the monetary statements of the Fed.

An average reading-grade-level of thirteen to fifteen years indicates that both statements are rather complex. However, as they address a professional audience, this should not raise problems. While the introductory statement has been relatively more standardized in language and length, the FOMC statements since the financial crisis have become considerably longer and more difficult to read (this has somewhat changed more recently).

These days central banks are trying to modernize their approaches to communication. They consider not only the readability of the language used but also the changing role of the media, with a substantial decline of trust in traditional channels and the spread of Twitter and similar online media as the main venues for market participants to discuss information (see Haldane 2017). The Bank of England, in joint research with psychologists, is attempting to capture sentiment in financial markets by applying semantic analysis techniques to the words used by market participants. On the other hand, such models and various text-mining techniques are also being applied to analyze the communication, words, and phrases used by central banks (Bholat et al. 2015).

All major central banks have substantially extended their communication departments. The use of language, psychological, and other experts and an attempt to elevate communication to a kind of applied science are common elements of this approach. Such a development, which tries to take into account relevant research from psychology to advertising, is anything but surprising, and might go even further. But can we be sure that such "science-based" communication will deliver better results in terms of the central bank's goals? Is there not a risk that such approaches, including the use of social media, might be perceived as attempts to "manage" expectations and perhaps even to manipulate a range of audiences? (See Coibion et al. 2018.)

It might be worthwhile considering past cases in which communication was seen as successful, though it violated almost all principles of modern central bank communication theory. An extreme example is provided by Alan Greenspan. Consider his remarks at a U.S. Senate hearing in 1987 (see Qvigstad and Schei 2018, 9). "Since becoming a central banker, I have learned to mumble with great incoherence. If I seem unduly clear to you, you must have misunderstood what I said."

As a biographer has noted,

Greenspan can subtly confound his audience. His congressional testimony is now televised on cable channels and his statements combed for meaning, but almost never does he surrender a sound bite. He does not provide a clear declaration about the condition of the economy or the likely direction of interest rates. His long, convoluted sentences seem to take away at the end what they have given at the beginning, as they flow to new levels of incomprehensibility. He uses what he calls "constructive ambiguity." (Woodward 2000, 227)

On the previous page the author of *Maestro* claims that "Greenspan's policy of expanding openness and transparency has done more than merely increase the Fed's accountability." The contradiction with the previous quotation is obvious. However, Woodward stresses that Greenspan focused attention on the Fed and himself. His personal credibility was so outstanding that the general public, and to a wide extent academics and financial observers, did not criticize this ambiguity but saw it more or less as an outstanding example of supporting trust in the person and the institution that he represented.

This example is mentioned not to claim that it could be a standard for communication. And times have changed anyway. However, Greenspan's case demonstrates that even ambiguous, incomprehensible statements can successfully provide information—provided that the sender is possessed of undisputed credibility.

This conclusion embodies a warning for overambitious attempts to make central bank communication a kind of applied science based on formal models. It will be interesting to see how progress in professional central bank communication can integrate reputational aspects. Does this imply limits to fine-tuning communication? How can trust in personalities be combined with requests for modern communication?

To what extent should the challenge of appropriate communication be a criterion when appointing central bank governors? (On the types of central bankers between 1950 and 2000, see Wendschlag 2018.) Ignoring these characteristics could have a negative impact on relations with markets and the general public. However, giving communication skills priority over knowledge and character might, over time, cause reputational damage to the central bank.

5 Communication and the Effectiveness of Monetary Policy

5.1 Guiding Expectations

The central bank, using its "normal" instruments, can only fix the central bank interest rate, and thereby control the very short end of the interest rate spectrum. Its influence on the long end depends on market expectations regarding future central bank decisions—and their expected impact on inflation (and other macroeconomic variables). Expectations are a key factor in the transmission of monetary policy to the economy. Woodford (2005) goes so far as to claim that very little else matters other than expectations about policy. In the long history of central banks, they have only recently professionalized their communication and adopted a wide range of tools.

The Bank deutscher Länder and its successor, the Deutsche Bundesbank, placed great emphasis on regular communication with the media and the broader public from the beginning, mainly through its *Monthly Bulletin*, which received nationwide coverage in the media. It would be wrong to suggest that central banks have ignored the importance of expectations for monetary policy in the past. Messages were more or less implicit, including references to their track record and an emphasis on their commitment to their mandate.

The years after German reunification (1989–1990) provide an interesting case. The macroeconomic situation was turned upside down. Public finances showed a high deficit, the current account went from surplus to deficit, and so on. The Bundesbank was exposed to strong pressure from all sides under these special, historically unique circumstances to be temporarily "less dogmatic" about its objective of maintaining price stability. The bank resisted these pressures and insisted that it was now even more important to remain committed to its mandate and gradually bring the level of inflation of more than 4 percent down to its implicit normative rate of 2 percent (see Issing 2005).

Reunification was a special situation, but the German central bank (including the Bank deutscher Länder as the predecessor of the Deutsche Bundesbank) had acquired its high reputation as guardian of the currency during a long process. This process was accompanied by overall communication. Reunification and its economic consequences represented a test of this credibility and the corresponding communication, as was proved by long-term interest rates remaining stable.

Nowadays central banks use a whole battery of communication tools to explain their policy. Among those communication tools, a few are aimed at guiding market expectations about future monetary policy. Here one can distinguish two dimensions. One entails sending signals in the run-up to monetary policy decisions (see the appendix to this book). This is the short-term dimension, focused on financial markets, which do not like to be surprised by the actions of the central bank.

In the past, "surprising the markets" was used by central banks from time to time as a tactic to demonstrate who was "the master of the game." It is hardly appropriate to increase uncertainty, however. If actors in financial markets feel they are being misguided by central bank communication, they will have lost money. As a consequence, they will be loud critics, with strong support from at least some sections of the media. Central banks might therefore be tempted to avoid the risk and to signal their intentions in a way that is seen as a kind of unconditional commitment. In such a case, either the credibility of upholding such commitments comes into doubt if the data and assessments change—a classic case of time inconsistency—or the appropriate monetary policy is compromised farther down the road.

The other dimension of communication on monetary policy relates to the medium to long term. A difficult challenge here is to provide consistency between the sequence of current decisions (and their communication) and the longer-term objectives of monetary policy. Without credibility gained over a considerable track record, this can hardly be achieved. Such credibility is based on following a strategy focused on fulfilling the mandate, being convincing about the commitment to this goal, and using appropriate communication. Financial markets (and as far as possible the general public) should have a clear understanding of how the central bank would react to exogenous shocks. In technical terms, the reaction function of the central bank should be transparent and convincing. This requirement is, however, especially hard to fulfill in a period of low or rather zero nominal central bank interest rates.

The Reserve Bank of New Zealand was the first to publish an interest rate path. It was followed by the central banks of Norway and Sweden. This form of guiding expectations is widely seen as state of the art. The pros—and less so the cons—of this approach have been the subject of numerous publications. However, here are a number of caveats to be observed. A crucial question is over what time horizon those forecasts can give reliable information. It is not surprising that uncertainty, and as a consequence "ex-post errors," increase over time, which shows that caution must be exercised (Goodhart and Lim 2011). Moreover, persistent deviations between published policy intentions and market expectations may raise questions about the central bank's credibility or induce excessive sensitivity to market perceptions (Shin 2017).

5.2   Forward Guidance: A Revolution in Communication?

Central bank communication developed in a long evolutionary process that mostly involved learning by doing rather than rational design. At the zero lower bound, traditional monetary policy instruments reached their limit (Bernanke 2013). Together with quantitative easing, forward guidance has been seen as the proper reaction to this challenge—a large leap forward in the previously steady evolution. Yellen (2012) even sees forward guidance as a revolution in central bank communication.

What is the essence of forward guidance?

With forward guidance, "the central bank communicates not only about the current setting of monetary policy, but makes explicit statements about the future path of policy" (Blinder et al. 2017). Central bank communication with the goal of guiding expectations to make monetary policy more effective was always focused on information about future actions by the central bank. Take the case of the Reserve Bank of New Zealand, which published the path of its future interest rates many years previously. Was this not already a clear case of forward guidance?

It is no accident that forward guidance as a specific communication strategy was "discovered" in the context of the zero lower bound for central bank interest rates. In such an environment, forward guidance is widely seen as the most important if not the only monetary policy instrument (see, e.g., Blinder et al. 2017). Central bank communication in normal times aims at making monetary policy—through instruments such as interest rate policies—more effective. Forward guidance, however, is nothing other than communication; communication itself becomes a monetary policy instrument. Weidmann (2018) extends this definition to central bank communication in general. In practice, forward guidance can be interpreted as communication that the central bank will keep its interest rates unchanged and/or will extend quantitative easing over a longer period, longer than markets would have otherwise expected, which means beyond the start of an economic recovery or a rise in the inflation rate from unwelcome low levels. However, it is necessary to caution against the view that communication offers a kind of additional "independent" monetary policy instrument, as ultimately any course of action announced will have to be validated and needs to remain consistent with the monetary policy strategy. Seen from this perspective, forward guidance could be used to strengthen communication regarding the reaction function of the central bank (Draghi 2014).

The appointment of Pompeius and its resulting economic effects, described in chapter 2, demonstrate that the impact of communication on expectations has a long history. So it is not surprising that a new nomenclature reflects this experience (Campbell et al. 2012). With "Odyssean forward guidance," the central bank commits itself, like Odysseus tying himself to the mast. In contrast, "Delphic forward guidance" is as ambiguous as the pronouncements of the famous oracle in ancient Greece as communication describes only the likely course of future monetary policy, depending on forecasts of economic developments. The new term, "Aesopian forward guidance" (Moessner, Jansen, and de Haan 2017), is an even less committal form of Delphic forward guidance, named after the fables of Aesop, through which the central bank announces that it will act episodically under unusual circumstances.

At the zero lower bound, the central bank would keep the policy rate at zero for some time after the point at which a forward-looking, inflation-targeting bank or a bank following a forward-looking Taylor rule would begin to raise interest rates (Woodford 2013). Starting from the zero lower bound, and with low levels of growth and inflation, one would expect forward guidance to become less important in the course of the recovery. In contrast, President Draghi stressed that "as a consequence of this continued expansion, also the component coming from the forward guidance of interest rates will gain further and further importance" (Draghi 2018). Does this mean that the ECB's already extreme expansionary policy of keeping its interest rate at (and below) zero and continuing quantitative easing—although with a lower amount—is further amplified? Is there not a risk that markets will interpret announcements of an "expected path" as an unconditional commitment?

In this context, it is important to distinguish different forms of forward guidance with respect to the degree of commitment (Delphic vs. Odyssean) and the form of conditionality (date-based vs. data-dependent).

So far, four different forms of forward guidance have been practiced (ECB 2014; Issing 2014):

1. *Pure qualitative forward guidance.* This approach includes neither an explicit end date, nor a numerical threshold, nor any explicit reference to the conditions that are relevant for a change in policy. A typical example is the announcement of the Fed in 2003 that "policy accommodation can be maintained for a considerable period" (FOMC 2003).

2. *Qualitative forward guidance conditional on a "narrative" about the macroeconomic conditions under which the present policy will prevail.* This is the approach preferred by the ECB until recently, in June 2018, when explicit data-based and state-contingent elements were strengthened—just at a time when the Fed was seeking to extricate itself from those forms of forward guidance.

3. *Calendar-based forward guidance.* This form was applied by the Fed when, on August 9, 2011, the terms of keeping the federal funds rate at low levels "for some time" and "an extended period of time" were replaced by "at least through mid-2013" (FOMC 2011).

4. *Outcome-based forward guidance explicitly sets numerical conditions for a future change in policy.* Again, the Fed can be taken as an example for defining an endpoint for the

continuation of the present policy: "At least as long as the unemployment rate remains above 6½ [percent], inflation between one and two years ahead is projected to be no more than a half point above the Committee's 2-percent longer-run goal, and longer-term inflation expectations continue to be well anchored" (Fed 2012). The Bank of England adopted outcome-based guidance in August 2013, conditional exclusively on a numerical threshold for unemployment, before announcing, in an update of February 2014, that it would take into account a broader range of indicators.

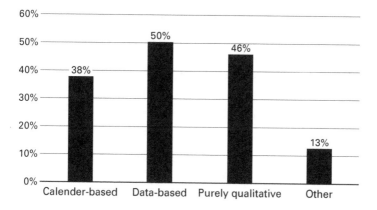

Figure 5.1

Types of forward guidance used in recent years. The vertical axis denotes the percentage of responding central bank heads. Graph is based on the replies of twenty-four governors whose central bank used forward guidance. Multiple answers were possible, and a total of thirty-five answers were received. *Source:* Alan S. Blinder et al., "Necessity As the Mother of Invention: Monetary Policy after the Crisis," ECB Working paper 2047 (Frankfurt am Main: European Central Bank, 2017).

The initial enthusiasm on the effectiveness of forward guidance has faded away and been replaced by a more modest assessment of its potential and its contradictions, notably when interpreted as a "commitment device." There would have been no need to test the idea of a calendar-based approach, as it is obvious that such precise timing is in stark contrast to the uncertainty of any forecast (see Feroli et al. 2017).

To a lesser degree, this is also true for outcome-based forward guidance. Data on unemployment, which are lagging indicators in any case and exposed to short-term volatility as well as to revision, can be influenced substantially by the participation rate. In the course of a recovery, discouraged workers might reenter the labor market, a kind of reversal of the previous hysteresis effect. The continuous decline in estimations for the U.S. natural rate of unemployment in recent years provides an impressive example of how difficult it is to announce a fixed number for the unemployment rate to call success and subsequently phase out expansionary monetary policy. (The experience of the Bank of England has also been striking, as the announced threshold for unemployment was quickly breached and practically abandoned.)

A comparable discussion can be had on the question of the extent to which new factors such as globalization and technical progress (e.g., the digital economy) have changed the dynamics of the domestic inflation rate. There are rather obvious arguments against the calendar-based and outcome-based options of forward guidance. But there are also critical aspects that relate to the theoretical basis of forward guidance in general. Forward guidance represents an attempt to exert an expansionary effect beyond reductions in the central bank interest rate, which finds its limit at the zero lower bound in any case. This effect of the announcement that the low central bank rate will remain in place for a longer period is produced through a reduction in the market nominal and real interest rates, which is in turn achieved by encouraging investors to shift their portfolios into longer maturities, thereby reducing long-term interest rates. Providing information on the future path of monetary policy is also intended to reduce uncertainty among investors, thereby also reducing volatility in the markets.

Low interest rates induce private actors to make riskier investments. Forward guidance encourages risk-taking beyond the level already achieved by low rates. Triggering such portfolio shifts is a risky strategy.

A new positive shock on output and inflation would bring the central bank into a difficult situation, and not least because investors in financial markets, having followed forward guidance, would suffer losses if the central bank were to raise its interest rates. Therefore, strong criticism would be triggered from actors in financial markets—and sections of the media—to which central banks are often inclined to give special attention. This might lead the central bank to hesitate with a rate hike, to delay or even cancel such a move, which would be all the more likely if the financial sector was not robust enough to digest these "central bank–induced losses." This shows "a fundamental problem of forward guidance: It suffers from the same sort of time inconsistency malaise that it seeks to remedy. Announcing that the policy rate will remain low well into the future does not imply that the central bank, from the perspective of a future date and in the face of rising inflation, will have an incentive to follow through on its commitment. The reason is, of course, that at that future moment, the central bank will be confronted with all the costs associated with keeping its promise, while all the benefits will already have been reaped. Therefore, forward guidance will be very prone to time inconsistency"—at least when understood as a commitment (Issing 2014).

The main goal of forward guidance is to reduce (if not exclude) uncertainty about future actions of the central bank. An inflation-targeting bank publishing the path of future central bank rates is regarded as (something of) a state-of-the-art approach. (Recent studies reveal a preference for price level targeting—see, e.g., Cole 2018.)

Here are three critical remarks on this approach, which apply in principle to all forms of forward guidance:

1. It is difficult to assess the impact of the announced interest rates on the economy. New shocks might hit the economy. Monetary policy is confronted with time lags, which can vary with the magnitude and type of shocks, the prevailing financial sentiment, and many other variables. This makes it impossible to precisely time the impact of policy action.

2. All economic forecasts are exposed to uncertainty. Central banks communicate uncertainty through fan charts or ranges. However, for outside observers it is not an easy task to assess this information correctly. Quite often, for the sake of simplicity, the average of a range is taken as a proxy. The announcement of future actions must under no circumstances take the form of an unconditional commitment. The Swedish central bank, for example, tries to make this clear when stressing the conditionality of the projected interest rate path: "It is a forecast—not a promise." The same applies to the famous "dots" published by the Fed. It remains an open question whether outside observers always take such warnings properly into account. Theory and practice might differ more often than not (Moessner, Jansen, and de Haan 2017).

Most publications in this context refer only to "uncertainty" and ignore the important distinction between "risk" and "uncertainty" drawn by Frank Knight: "At the heart of modern macroeconomics is the … illusion that uncertainty can be confined to the mathematical manipulation of known probabilities" (King 2016a, 121).

What would be left of the pretension of forward guidance efficiency once radical, that is, Knightian, uncertainty was respected?

3. The central bank is exposed in its policy to risk and uncertainty. This raises a more than logical challenge of how far the central bank, being aware of the problems of forecasting, can reduce public uncertainty in the perception of its communication.

Empirical studies on the efficiency of forward guidance so far deliver at best limited evidence (Blinder et al. 2017; Moessner, Jansen, and de Haan 2017). All results have to be taken with a grain of salt, mainly because of the identification problems. But, even if one assumes that forward guidance is effective in guiding expectations and that the central bank will meet its inflation target, price stability is not enough. It can be accompanied by large variations in real activity (Woodford 2013). Inflation targeting ignores the development of money and credit and financial stability in general. However, ultimately this is not an argument against forward guidance as such but against a monetary policy strategy based on forecasts, which suffer significantly from this neglect, or at best limited consideration, of monetary and financial aspects.

It is too early to come to a definitive conclusion about forward guidance as a specific form of central bank communication. As already mentioned, the initial enthusiasm over this "revolution" in central bank communication has more or less disappeared. Departing from the zero lower bound will deprive forward guidance of its special necessity as the only remaining monetary policy instrument. In the end, the term "forward guidance" might remain, but the meaning will be reduced to the state of normal communication to guide expectations with the aim of making monetary policy more effective.

5.3   Communication and Committee Structure

For a long time—and not only in textbooks—monetary policy decisions were perceived as acts by a single person. Accordingly, the headlines read along the lines of "Greenspan raises interest rates" or "Draghi keeps interest rates low." In some cases in the past, the governor had de jure internally unlimited authority or dominated de facto in such a way that the news reflected reality. Over time, however, things have changed, and all major central banks make decisions by committee. Their structure differs widely. Voting rights might rotate (the Federal Open Market Committee [FOMC], the ECB); committee members might come from central bank districts (the Fed) or different nations (the ECB), from inside or outside the central bank, and so on. Although the efficiency of a committee may depend on its size, the general consensus is that a committee structure is more suitable than a single "dictator." These aspects are important but will not be discussed further.

The focus here is on the consequences of a committee structure for central bank communication (see, e.g., Qvigstad and Schei 2018).

In this context the committee structure is primarily seen as a risk to effective communication. This starts with the discussion and decision-making process. A monetary policy decision might have been made before different members' views have been fully discussed and taken on board. In other words, the central bank's reaction function, which expresses the committee's understanding, is incomplete (Stein 2014). This makes proper communication of the reasoning behind the decision rather difficult.

For an interesting example, see the minutes of the Swedish central bank's Executive Board meeting of September 1, 2010:

Mr. Svensson believed that the repo rate path in the main scenario is unreasonably high. It is far above market expectations and the corresponding short-term and long-term market rates. If it were to achieve full credibility, market expectations would shift upwards to the same degree. This would have fateful consequences. Mr. Svensson called on his colleagues on the Executive Board to point out any faults in his reasoning.... Normally, the Riksbank's wish and endeavor is that the repo rate path shall gain credibility and be incorporated into market expectations and market pricing. In this way, monetary policy will have the largest possible impact. However, this time it is the opposite. Mr. Svensson claimed that if the repo rate path in the main scenario is supported by the majority (of the board), one must hope that it is still not credible and thus will not have very large consequences before it can hopefully be corrected at the next monetary policy meeting. There is an old saying that one should be careful what one wishes for. This is because getting what you wished for may sometimes have unforeseen consequences. This could be one of those times. Mr. Svensson claimed that in this case, one should not wish for better credibility for the repo rate path. (Sveriges Riksbank 2010)

The ECB makes monetary policy decisions by consensus. This procedure was initially widely misinterpreted by outside observers, as can be demonstrated by the following example. When, in April 1999, the ECB lowered the central bank policy rates by 50 basis points and raised them by 50 points half a year later, these actions were widely interpreted as the expression of a tortuous discussion process in a heterogeneous group that was ultimately forced to make such sizable changes to interest rates (see Issing 2008, 154). When, at a later stage, 25 basis point changes were decided on, this was deemed to be the expression of a timid policy, again typical for such a group that finds it hard to decide on large interest rate changes.

Just because of the complex structure of the Governing Council, information on the monetary policy decision was (wrongly) perceived as a kind of implicit communication on the difficulties of reaching decisions.

The ECB's consensus principle, however, had a clear rational background. Consensus has never been seen as waiting until every member expresses the same preference. It is enough that a majority is in favor of a certain action, which in the end should be supported by every member, even by those who initially preferred not to act in this way. Having "lost" in a vote might undermine this willingness to support the action.

The special communication challenge for the ECB, which took over responsibility for the new currency, the euro, on January 1, 1999, was all too obvious to the public. (The language problem is only mentioned.) A committee comprising six members of the board and eleven governors from national central banks was widely perceived as too heterogeneous to come to appropriate monetary decisions for the euro area. Despite this background, I urged President Willem Duisenberg to organize a press conference immediately after a monetary policy meeting. Initially Duisenberg was very reluctant, if not hostile to this idea. But I finally convinced him by pointing to the risk of what might happen otherwise. National central bank governors would present the result to their national audiences, and, absent strong guidance from the center, a cacophony would be unavoidable.

The ECB was criticized from the beginning for not publishing minutes, including votes on monetary policy decisions (Buiter 1999). The arguments on the side of the ECB mainly referred to the special political and economic environment the central bank faced (Issing 1999), and the statute (Article 10.4) stipulates that the proceedings of the meetings are confidential. (The Governing Council may decide to make the outcome of its deliberations public.)

A committee structure makes communication an extremely difficult task for any central bank. Even with best intentions, it is almost impossible to "speak with one voice." A central bank that speaks in a cacophony of voices may have "no voice at all" (Lustenberger and Rossi 2017b). However, it might be worse, as such diverging communication will create confusion. The influence of individual members on the internal discussion and decision-making process might differ widely. Accordingly, the public will have great difficulty weighing the different voices in the communication process. Opponents to the decision made might get undue attention. Conversely, communication by individual members with opinions differing from the majority's could be used to exert pressure on the decision-making body. The success of such dissenters will depend on the specific circumstances.

There will be circumstances in which dissenting views continue and become part of the overall picture. Once a single committee member comes out with a statement beyond the "official line," that member might be corrected by the bank[1]—probably explaining that the member's remarks were "misinterpreted."

The potential reaction to outside communication by individual members, the committee, or the chairman on the internal discussion and decision-making process is hardly discussed. But is it not almost naïve to separate, for example, voting from the following communication? Is it out of the question that an individual member might vote exactly this way and not otherwise because of the effect of the following public information? Motives could be very diverse. Intention to draw public attention? Conforming with the majority to avoid being seen as an outsider? Voting with the chairman to support his authority—or exactly the opposite?

The experience with the Monetary Policy Committee of the Bank of England demonstrates the trade-offs stemming from a committee structure:

It should be clear that there are both benefits and costs to a group decision-making process. The transparency and account-

---

1. On April 1, 2018, the German financial newspaper *Börsen-Zeitung* carried the headline "EZB pfeift Euro-Notenbanker Nowotny zurück" (ECB brings euro central banker Nowotny back into line).

ability of individual views help to make better decisions. But it also complicates the communication of the decision to a wider audience, whose expectations of inflation matter for economic behavior. The avoidance of confusion requires some forebearance by individual members of the Committee, and a clear understanding of which forms of communication are appropriate to explain individual views and which forms are suitable for explaining the reasons for a collective decision. (King 2002)

Individual members should in principle feel obliged to restrain personal ambitions and refrain from dissenting statements. If, on the other hand, a fundamental and lasting dissent exists, would it not be a moral obligation to go public?

5.4   Communication and Financial Markets

The central bank communicates with very different audiences. But financial markets are its most important target. The basic intention is to influence, through communication, market expectations that monetary policy can be made more effective.

For many reasons, however, this is a complex and demanding challenge. First of all, communication is not a one-way endeavor. The central bank not only influences financial markets, it also takes information from them (Morris and Shin 2018). Because of this mutual influence, information coming from markets is not "pure" market information but is "spoiled" by the influence exerted by the central bank's communication. The consequence is a feedback loop. Samuelson (1994) refers to the experience of a monkey who sees himself in a mirror for the first time. Accordingly, the chairman receives from the market what the market heard the chairman saying before. "Central Banks become echo chambers of their own making" (Shin 2017). The markets react to the central bank's communication, digest the signals, and transform the conjecture about future monetary policy into investment decisions. The consequences are reflected in financial variables, which enter the assessment of the central bank and can influence its policy decisions, and so forth. For Jeremy Stein (2014, 9), QE3 illustrates the fact that the FOMC's reaction function has been shaped by market responses, and vice versa. It was not only evolving over time but "coevolving along with the market belief."

Forward guidance can amplify this feedback loop. This is because forward guidance influences inflation expectations and can trigger—as intended by the central bank— moves in market prices because of front-running by market participants. The signal, the "echo" from market prices, can also be amplified, "reverberating in an echo chamber of its own. In the worst case, the central bank may end up in a feedback loop where acting on signals from the market could distort the signals further" (Morris and Shin 2018, 3) In this context, it is also relevant that "the market" is not one person, but is composed of many actors. Those actors can be very heterogeneous and have different preferences, for example in relation to risk-taking. "Optimists" may react strongly on forward guidance (Stein 2014) and may sell assets with short maturities, which will have to be bought by less optimistic actors. This heterogeneity of actors in financial markets may therefore cause an amplifying effect of forward guidance, which could have a reverse effect once monetary policy, current or expected, changes. Higher volatility will result, including the risk of greater market turbulence.

Central banks today invest large amounts of resources in research and statistics—and are supposed to be reliable and honest in their information policy. However, this does not guarantee that central bank information is always superior to information from private sources. This implies the risk that in some cases public communication, in this case by the central bank, crowds out private information, thereby reducing welfare (Morris and Shin 2002). The debate on the relevance of this effect in general is ongoing (Morris and Shin 2006; Svensson 2006; Lustenberger and Rossi 2017a). In the context of communication on monetary policy, it seems not unlikely that central bank communication, which is unavoidably exposed to uncertainty, may have a bias related to its strategy and policy implementation. A striking example is the output gap, which is one of the most elusive indicators to estimate in real time (Orphanides 2011). Forecast inflation targeting relies on output gap data, for which a variety of figures are usually available. It is hard to believe that the choice of data is independent of the monetary policy intentions of the central bank.

Research in this field is costly. Private resources may not be competitive with central banks' research and will in any case have difficulties gaining adequate attention with diverging views.

It is not only the information about data as such—what also matters is the weight given to various data, from interest rates, spreads, and so on to monetary or credit aggregates. Remember what Deputy Governor Harvey said: "Undue importance might be given to certain things that are stated, more importance than perhaps they merit" (see Macmillan 1931, 27).

Finally, there can be a misguiding element in central bank communication that is hardly given any attention. If, for example, the central bank announces that it will not change its interest rate for some time to come, there is a great risk that this will be perceived as an unchanged path of monetary policy. This impression is further strengthened by references to a "steady hand course." However, this information is misleading, and the perception by market participants is wrong or at least biased. A continuing recovery—reducing the output gap—would demand a change in the central bank's interest rate to apply an unchanged monetary policy stance. It depends on the situation whether the misperception of a "steady hand" has a relevant impact on the behavior of actors in financial markets.

Central bank communication with financial markets is a highly complex challenge. Financial markets are a key element in the transmission of monetary policy to the economy, employment, and prices. The reactions of actors in these markets are important not only for the impact of monetary policy decisions. At the same time, "dissatisfaction" in the market with central bank actions and communication will be expressed quickly and loudly. As a consequence of these interactions, there is a temptation, if not a tendency, for central banks to give financial markets more weight than might be appropriate. Alan Blinder's (1998, 76) warning is today more relevant than ever: "Following the markets too closely … may lead the central bank to inherit precisely the short term horizon that central bank independence is meant to prevent. There is no more reason for central bankers to take their marching orders from bond traders than to take their orders from politicians."

6   Communication and Accountability

Like all public institutions in a democracy, although to a different degree, central banks are accountable. "An accountable bank must give account, explain and justify the actions or decisions taken, against criteria of some kind, and take responsibility for any fault or damage" (Goodhart and Lastra 2017).

Modern central banks are established by an act of the legislature and exert their powers according to the law and/or instructions from the government. This is also the legal basis for the appointment of the governor and board members or committees with executive power.

Those legal acts provide the legitimacy of the central bank. Legitimacy preexists and is the requisite of accountability. Beyond this formal character, legitimacy is also based on support from the public. Legitimacy and accountability are interdependent: no legitimacy without accountability, no accountability without legitimacy.

Because of the comprehensive guarantee of independence (see Siekmann 2013), Article 130 AEUV, the European

System of Central Banks (ESCB), its components, and its organs are accountable only to the extent explicitly provided for in the primary law of the EU. The ECB, for example, must present an annual report covering the activities of the Eurosystem and the monetary policy of both the previous and the current year (ECB 2002a, 2018). The complex character of the EU is reflected in the number of addressees: the European Parliament, the EU Commission, the EU Council, and the European Council. The treaty also calls for the publication of quarterly reports. The annual report is presented to the plenary of the European Parliament by the president of the ECB. The president also appears four times a year before the Committee on Economic and Monetary Affairs of the European Parliament. These testimonies have become the core of the European Parliament's role in holding the ECB accountable. Other board members may also be invited to appear by this committee.

Most central banks have similar obligations to report and testify. For instance, the appearance of the chairman of the Federal Reserve Board before the committees of both the U.S. House of Representatives and the Senate to discuss the semiannual reports usually gains high attention from the public.

Central banks are free to go beyond legal obligations, and most of them do. The Eurosystem may, however, only do so within the limits of the confidentiality of the meetings (Article 10.4 of the statute) and professional secrecy (Article 37 of the statute).

Accountability to inform and explain is an obvious responsibility and does not raise problems. This is in contrast to the request to "justify" the actions and decisions of an independent central bank. The central banks of the ESCB are endowed with the statute of independence to make monetary policy decisions free from any political pressure or interference. Article 130 (AEUV) stipulates:

When exercising the powers and carrying out the tasks and duties conferred upon them by this Treaty and the Statute of the ESCB, neither the ECB, nor a national central bank, nor any member of their decision-making bodies shall seek or take instructions from Community institutions or bodies, from any government of a Member State or from any other body. The Community institutions and bodies and the government of the Member States undertake to respect this principle and not to seek to influence the members of the decision-making bodies of the ECB or of the national central banks in the performance of their tasks.

This very explicit text reflects concerns about potential interference from any political or societal institution and protects the ESCB's independence as far as one could go in a legal text. Even the mere attempt to influence the decision-making process is prohibited. At the same time, it makes clear that independence is limited to "exercising power" and carrying out "tasks and duties conferred" by the treaty and the statute. Thus it is functionally limited. On monetary policy, this means within the limits of the tasks and competences laid down in Article 127 AEUV.

A central bank that is given full independence by the legislator—as in the case of the ECB—does not have to "justify" its actions and decisions (within its mandate) in a legal sense. In other words, these activities are not exposed to judicial control. This may be illustrated by a famous example from 1981, when the FOMC based its case for not publishing policy directives and minutes on arguments from monetary and financial theory (see Issing 2005).

To the judge it was "apparent, however, upon reviewing the affidavits that the dispute among the experts in this case [was] not one over facts in any objective sense, but rather [was] a dispute over economic theory. It may in fact be finally reducible to a dispute over proper monetary policy." Consequently, the judge ruled that "insofar as judgements pertaining to the validity of a particular policy are entrusted to the FOMC under the auspices of Congress, the Court lacks the expertise necessary to substitute its judgement or that of plaintiffs' experts for that of the FOMC."

This judgment would presumably also be given in case a court had to decide on the "lawfulness" of a monetary policy decision. An independent central bank is not accountable to justify its decisions in a legal sense. "Justifying" could only mean explaining why certain monetary policy decisions were taken (see Qvigstad and Schei 2018). (However, it must be kept in mind that the independence of the Federal Reserve System—in contrast to the ESCB—is not protected by the U.S. Constitution but only in much weaker form by the Federal Reserve Act.)

Endowing appointed, "unelected technocrats" with the power to make decisions that are so important for society has been discussed for a long time. The pros and cons fill libraries (Tucker 2018). For the situation in Germany, see Issing (1993).

There is a broad if not unanimous consensus that the independence of central banks must be limited by a clear mandate, which is price stability or low inflation. A dual mandate, which usually includes a high level of employment, widens the powers as well as the explicit responsibility of the central bank and may blur the dividing line between monetary policy and economic policies that fall within the government's remit. This is not the place to discuss the pros and cons of a single versus a dual mandate. This issue is elaborated by Yellen (2012, 10–11): "Given that the rate of inflation in the longer run is determined solely by monetary policy, central banks can, and indeed must, determine the long-run level of inflation. In contrast, they cannot do much to affect the sustainable maximum level of employment." This does not, however, relieve the central bank of the obligation to specify also the second goal within the dual mandate. The Fed has decided to couch the employment goal in terms of the unemployment rate. However, there is considerable disagreement even within the FOMC on the longer-run normal level of unemployment—and this assessment can change in the course of time. (As already mentioned, in the statement of December 2011 the threshold for a change in its monetary policy at that time was an unemployment rate of 6½ percent! In the following years this rate was continuously and substantially revised downward.)

Whereas a central bank with a single mandate, price stability, cannot ignore this issue, communication in the context of a dual mandate is confronted with a tremendous challenge.

Central bank independence is increasingly under threat from these developments:

1. Every monetary policy decision will have distributional effects. These are unavoidable and a kind of unintended side effect. A very different case is when the central bank adopts instruments with a special distributional effect. These are measures like providing cheap credit to special groups, banks, companies, or households (e.g., student loans), which have direct and intentional discriminatory effects. Decisions of this kind cannot be among the competencies and responsibilities of an independent central bank. They must remain firmly in the realm of politics, which is ultimately accountable to the voters.

2. Coordination with fiscal policy is a minefield for independent central banks. In the case of implementation of instruments that are de facto acts of fiscal policy, the central bank will be exposed to criticism that it is exceeding its competencies. If the central bank yields to political pressure, though independence might still be legally untouched, de facto it will be undermined or even abandoned. The central bank could hardly argue that it is not accountable for such activities.

3. Since the financial crisis, many central banks have been given additional competencies in the field of micro-

and macroprudential policies. If the tasks of the central bank are expanded by the competence for banking supervision, this might lead to interrelations with fiscal policies undermining independence and conflicts with the conduct of monetary policy to fulfill its primary objective of maintaining price stability (de Larosière et al. 2009). Again, the call for accountability would have a different character than in the case of monetary policy.

4. Overburdening of central banks has become a severe threat to independence (Issing 2017).

One reason is exaggerated expectations of what central banks can achieve. The "Great Moderation" as a period of low inflation and a rather strong economy was widely seen as a result of sound monetary policy. Central bank reputation increased further after the banks had, in line with fiscal policy, saved the world from falling from the Great Recession into a depression as in the 1930s. "The extraordinary burden placed on central banking since the crisis is generating growing strains. During the Great Moderation, markets and the public at large came to see central banks as all-powerful. Post-crisis, they have come to expect the central bank to manage the economy, restore full employment, ensure strong growth, preserve price stability and foolproof the financial system. But in fact, central banks alone cannot deliver. The extraordinary measures taken to stimulate the global economy have sometimes tested the boundaries of the institution. As a consequence, risk to its reputation, perceived legitimacy and independence have been rising" (BIS 2016, 22). Such elevated expectation over time must be disappointed, which in turn will extract a heavy price in reputation. It is always important for central banks to explain what they can do—and what not!—but now the challenge for communication is tougher than ever (see also Tucker 2018, 538).

Second, a central bank can substantially increase this threat by expanding its own interpretation of its tasks, objective, or competence. "The question of excessive reach, that is whether central banks have abrogated to themselves powers which are not in the mandate, and the legal interpretation of whether a central bank is abiding by the mandate or exceeding its powers, are fundamental issues in a democratic system" (Goodhart and Lastra 2017).

The ECB is a very special case of overburdening. This overburdening unfolded in the course of the euro area crisis in 2010, when the ECB embarked on a political exercise by buying government bonds of countries that otherwise might have been exposed to substantial increases in interest rates on their long-term bonds.

These selective interventions in the bond market were aimed at solving or at least mitigating the problems of some countries and raised questions as to whether these activities of the ECB may have violated the prohibition against monetary financing of sovereign budgets, which is enshrined in Article 123 AEUV. This issue became even more relevant after President Draghi announced in July 2012 that the ECB "is ready to do whatever it takes to preserve the euro," adding, "within our mandate." The following announcement of the OMT program specified what the ECB would do in the event of a future severe crisis. The case was brought before the German Constitutional Court and the European Court of Justice.

This is not the place for a thorough discussion of this complex case (see, e.g., Siekmann, Vig, and Wieland 2015). The fundamental question is, can a central bank simply declare such an action as "within its mandate"—that is, an act of monetary policy to maintain price stability? What are the limits of the justification of the announcement of such an unusual measure? Is this a measure to bypass the prohibition of monetary financing under the "disguise of monetary policy" (Schmidt 2015)? The case before the two courts and the courts' decisions provide a mixture of legal and economic arguments. Is it enough that the ECB declares an action as "within its mandate"—which implies no accountability in a legal sense when implementing the announced measures? The ECB has explained that those measures might be necessary to preserve the working of the monetary transmission mechanism. This is an interpretation with a large latitude and might come close to a kind of sovereignty to widen its mandate.

The German Federal Constitutional Court, in its judgment to refer the case to the European Court of Justice for a preliminary ruling, rejected this view and assessed the OMT to be an act of economic policy beyond the competencies of the ECB and to be monetary financing of sovereign debt, which is prohibited by the European Treaty.

In the end, the European Court of Justice followed the ESCB's economic interpretation of the OMT without further scrutiny. It is hard to understand the economic logic behind the legal argumentation presented at the courts.

Mervyn King's understanding is very different:

The proposal for outright monetary transactions is a transfer from countries that can borrow cheaply to countries that can't borrow cheaply. There's no point dressing up with fancy language such as measures to improve the transmission mechanism of monetary policy. It's a straight transfer from countries that have credibility in their ability to run their public finances to countries that don't. From that perspective, it clearly violates the no-bail clause of the European Treaty, and it runs completely counter to this vision of the monetary union. (King 2016b, 47)

The following statement by former vice president of the ECB Vitor Constâncio (on the OMT and other crisis management measures) gives a very different message than just preserving the working of the monetary policy transmission mechanism: "All the bold decisions taken during the crisis would not have been possible without the courageous leadership of President Jean-Claude Trichet and Mario Draghi and it was my privilege to work as Vice-President with both throughout these eventful years. Those decisions saved the euro area and illustrate the importance of having leaders with their convictions at the helm of the ECB" (Constâncio 2018).

Saviors of the euro area? Maybe. By acts of monetary policy? Hard to understand. What kind of convictions? In any case, were these activities within the mandate of the ECB? So far OMT has not been practiced. Figure 2.1 demonstrates the immediate announcement effect. But "whatever it takes" has a much longer and deeper impact. The announcement of OMT was a "game-changer"; it led to a new bond-pricing regime characterized by a weakened link between spreads and fiscal fundamentals (Afonso et al. 2018).

The ECB exemplifies the extraordinary power of a central bank. In general, objections to the independence of a central bank will grow exponentially with the extension of its powers. Calls for accountability will grow and will unavoidably extend to the core competence and responsibility of conducting monetary policy to maintain price stability. The threat to the bank's independent status increases in parallel with the growth in power.

Just to complete the aspects of accountability, one must distinguish between individual accountability of board members and collective accountability (see, e.g., ECB 2002a). Another challenge is to what extent an independent central bank should extend its communication to a field more or less far beyond the sphere of monetary policy. Willem Buiter (2014) is very critical on central bankers using or rather misusing the high profile and visibility they have acquired in their office at the central bank to comment in their official position on issues far from their mandates and competence.

Central bank independence is always debated, and today is under specific threat. This implies a huge challenge for communication. "For CBI to be sustainable, society must support it.... That requires debate, and so scrutiny; it depends on performance, but also on reasons. Whether we think of them as wise and virtuous or as purely self-interested, sensible central bankers will want to invest in *reasoned* debate and criticism of their policies" (Tucker 2018, 422).

7 Communication and Transparency

Transparency is another goal of central bank communication. The call for transparency concerns all public institutions in a democracy. (Transparency has also become essential in business; examples here are information to be given to markets to prevent insider trading or to inform about ethical or environmental standards.)

Central banks cannot be generally exempted from such duties, although confidentiality and professional secrecy mark some limits because of the special responsibility of central banks (Braun 2017) and are required by legal provisions (Articles 10.4 and 37 of the statute). Rules for transparency have been extended and become legal obligations on a worldwide basis. Those rules include access to documents and similar requirements. The call for publication of the diaries of members of the Executive Board of the ECB was triggered by a closed meeting of a member with a group of investors that involved specific information. To prevent any impression of privileged access to market-relevant information, the publication of diaries might be a useful step. However, there are limits to formalizing this kind of accountability. In the end, it is the honesty of central bankers that forms the basis of trust in avoiding any misbehavior.

Interaction with actors in financial markets can take many forms. A recent study (Finer 2018), for example, finds evidence of a significant spike in taxi rides from the major commercial banks to the New York Fed immediately after the midnight lifting of a communication blackout imposed on the Fed staff.

Transparency is an obligation concerning all responsibilities and activities of a central bank as a public institution. Communication is the tool to achieve transparency and accountability. Communication, accountability, and transparency are interconnected in a kind of triad.

The focus here is on transparency of monetary policy. In a narrow sense, transparency can be interpreted as openness toward the amount and precision of information (Winkler 2000). In a broader sense, transparency goes beyond simple openness and is aimed at creating a genuine understanding of monetary policy, which necessitates clarity in the information given to the public. "Transparency can be defined as an environment in which the central bank provides in an open, clear and timely manner all relevant information on its mandate, strategy, assessments and policy decisions as well as its procedures to the general public and the markets. Transparency is ultimately about the genuine understanding by the public of the entire process of monetary policy making" (ECB

2002b, 59). It follows immediately from this definition that, while delivering on the goal of transparency, the central bank uses the information to make monetary policy more effective.

Probably the biggest challenge facing the central bank is how to deal with the uncertainty to which the central bank's monetary policy is exposed. (See also section 5.2, "Forward Guidance.") One way is to publish forecasts in the form of fan charts or ranges, or to present alternative scenarios for the interest rate path. Constructing those forecasts becomes unavoidably complex and brings the need for clarity of information to its limits. At the same time, this kind of transparency can only be aimed at professional audiences. How to communicate the recognized uncertainty to the general public remains a special challenge.

The credibility of the central bank is based on transparency in general and on its information policy in particular. Credibility of the latter rests on honesty in providing information (Winkler 2000). The ECB delivers an instructive example of the fundamental difficulties that may arise in this context. The decision on the appointment of members of the Executive Board and the decision that eleven countries would form the euro area were made just a few weeks before the ECB was established on June 1, 1998. Only seven months were left to prepare for the launch of the euro, a strategy, the operational framework, communication tools, and so forth. The lack of data on the euro area was tremendous. Having been responsible for the department of Economics (and Research), I still remember those days when I received (besides monetary aggregates) practically no relevant and reliable data on the overall picture of what would become the euro area, the area for which we would take over monetary policy responsibility in January of the following year. Data on unemployment, for example, were aggregated by Eurostat on the basis of information coming from individual member states that applied very different methods and time lags. And this is just one example. On top of the lack of current information, no time series existed to judge new data against the experience of the past. Models for the euro area still had to be developed; any forecast was exposed to extreme uncertainty. The introduction of a new currency, the move from national currencies to the euro, was an example of an extreme regime shift, which might imply a breakdown of structural relations (Lucas 1976). Overall, the ECB was confronted with uncertainty of all kinds—on data, parameters, models (Issing et al. 2001).

Under these circumstances, how can transparency be achieved through clarity of information? Would honesty not have demanded that the public be informed about how the ECB would have to start monetary policy for such a heterogeneous economic area under such a high degree of all kinds of uncertainty? How could a new central bank without any track record claim credibility? Being "honest" in a simple sense would have frightened the public by revealing information on all the problems and would have spoiled the launch. The ECB chose the only promising way out of this dilemma by announcing a strategy a whole ten weeks before the start, including a number to aid understanding of the mandate to maintain price stability—an annual rate of inflation below 2 percent to be achieved over the medium term. The strategy was presented as a robust approach appropriate for this historically unique situation.

Judged by the successful launch of the euro and the takeover of monetary policy responsibility, the ECB's communication was successful. Criticism of a lack of transparency was more or less limited to a few academic voices (Buiter 1999) and some media outlets. Evidently, the public and the markets had been convinced by the information from the ECB. It is hard to define honesty, but this example can be seen as a successful approach because the central bank had gained credibility not through a track record but through convincing communication. Trust in personalities will have also played a role.

Remembering Deputy Governor Harvey's answer (See p.4)—"We leave our actions to explain our policy"—central bank transparency has come a long way. Central banks were mainly driven by "demand" for more transparency, including legal requirements. Does this one-way development end in unlimited transparency? Central banks inform on their decisions, the strategy and the reasons behind them, and so on. The request for minutes includes information on voting and the like. Thinking ahead, unlimited transparency could end in regular live TV broadcasts of council meetings and similar activities.

There are obvious objections to such transparency. Discussions and predecisions would in this case shift outside the public meetings. Yet, if one accepts the postulate of absolute transparency, the issue is simply one of legal enforceability (see Issing 2005). Pushed further, unlimited transparency would include information on all reasoning behind individual voting and other decisions.

Unlimited transparency is a mirage. More and more transparency might even backfire by overloading the public with information. This could even be used as a tactic by the central bank. By doing so, the central bank might fulfill formal requests for transparency but violate the principles of clarity and honesty—and the goal of making monetary policy more effective.

There clearly exists a trade-off between the degree of transparency and other goals of communication. Not surprisingly, an empirical study shows that, starting from a very low level, increasing transparency has strong positive effects, while these returns decrease as transparency is extended further (Ehrmann et al. 2012).

A telling example is afforded by the production and publication of minutes. The title of such a product gives the impression that if you read the minutes you will get a reasonably thorough block of information, as if you had attended the meeting. However, minutes published by central banks are far from that. This is well illustrated by the objections raised when the FOMC, at its meeting on January 27–28, 2004, discussed whether the time lag before publication of the minutes should be reduced from six weeks to three (which was in fact done): "Some members raised concern, however, that accelerated release of the minutes might have the potential to feed back adversely on the deliberations of the Committee and on the minutes themselves. The members also emphasized the importance of allowing sufficient time for them to review and comment on the minutes and for reconciling differences of opinion among the members of a large and geographically dispersed Committee" (FOMC 2004).

In case meetings are recorded and the records are published later, this could be seen as establishing full transparency ex post. However, such transparency would come at a high price. Everybody would be aware that the presentation of written statements would come across far more professionally than oral, sometimes spontaneous contributions. The negative impact on the discussion and decision-making process would be a high price, probably too high. The trade-off becomes evident (see Meyer 2004). Having records published later might have a disciplining as well as a distortionary effect (on experiences at the Fed, see Hansen, McMahon, and Prat 2018).

The request for absolute, unlimited transparency has instinctive appeal, and any doubts raised against it are easily discarded as the intention to "hide" useful information from the public. On the other hand, unlimited transparency remains a mirage, and the path heading in this direction gives rise to many negative side effects. Transparency as a concept, as a moral and legal obligation, must not be seen in isolation. Transparency is not a means in itself (Mishkin 2004).

In their endeavor to satisfy the request for ever greater transparency, central banks have already gone very far.

When, for example, President Draghi in his press conference of September 13, 2018, was asked about details of the future of the bond-buying program, he answered: "We haven't even discussed when we're going to discuss it." The *Economist* (September 20, 2018) saw this statement as one of the "occasional absurdities" of central banks giving fine-grained forward guidance and as a case of transparency becoming almost comical. The reaction of the media on this topic might be very volatile, but even they seem to recognize the limits of reasonable transparency.

The demand for "full transparency" is a general phenomenon that addresses all activities in a society. Doctors are a special target. Giovanni Maio (2017), for example, complains about a "transparency dictate for surgeons," which does not lead to better surgery but to strong investment of energy in communication to the outside and the endeavor to optimize the impression on the public.

This can also be a risk for central banks. Transparency is an obligation in a democratic society to make an independent central bank accountable and contribute to the effectiveness of its monetary policy. It is impossible to draw a fixed line for the implicit trade-off. However, the dynamics of demands for more transparency are such that it would be hard to go back once it turned out that certain measures of transparency had gone too far.

8 Concluding Remarks

Central bank communication has gone on a long journey from close to zero information to a high degree of transparency and accountability, from a kind of amateurish ad hocery to professionalism. And this will be not the end of the story. New media, for example, might bring a major change, the effect of which cannot yet be predicted.

In politics, governments frequently claim: Our policy is good—but communication failed to make this success understood by the public, the voters. There is a risk that central banks, in the same sense, regard communication as a priority. However, monetary policy comes first—the tail must not wag the dog. Expecting central banks to ever reach the general public in an all-encompassing way, using every information channel from town hall meetings to TV, is an illusion. There are limits to this ambition (see also Blinder 2018).

Ultimately, the general public can only be convinced by a monetary policy that delivers stable money. In times of low inflation, it is no easy task to keep the inflationary threat alive in people's minds. It's the same as with freedom—one gets used to it and takes this precious gift for granted, which undermines resistance to detrimental developments.

Communication must not be blurred by all kinds of additional tasks and political considerations. The central message must always be: for us at the central bank the stability of our currency always has priority. (A dual mandate creates a special challenge for communication.) And monetary policy decisions must convince the people that the central bank will deliver on its mandate. Sound monetary policy and appropriate communication must go hand in hand. Matching deeds to words is the basis for credibility (Blinder 2000, 1422) on which the success of the central bank's actions finally rests.

Appendix

Table A.1
Communication: Instruments, Channels, and Target Groups

Instruments	Format	Channels	When
Immediate announcement/explanation of monetary policy decisions			
Press releases	Written	Website/ hard copy	Immediately after the monetary policy meeting
Press conference	Verbal, with question-and-answer session; sometimes includes distribution of written background information (e.g., opinion of the central bank president, projections) to media representatives	Direct communication, TV broadcast (live or report later that day)	Shortly after the monetary policy meeting
Transcript of the press conference	Written	Website/ hard copy	Shortly after the press conference has finished
Supplementary information on monetary policy decisions			
Publication of minutes of meetings	Written	Website/ hard copy	Between 13 days and 8 weeks after the monetary policy meeting
Publication of voting behavior	Written	Website/ hard copy	Together with the press release and/or minutes of the meeting

Frequency	Detail	Content	Target group
Regularly	Brief; in some cases information is reduced to key words and formulas	Monetary policy decision, sometimes including a brief explanation; monetary policy intentions; announcement of voting behavior	General public, media, markets
Regularly	Extensive	Explanation of the monetary policy decision; assessment of the current economic situation and its future development; sometimes comments on other policy areas	General public, media, markets
Regularly	Extensive	Explanation of the monetary policy decision; assessment of the current economic situation and its future development; sometimes comments on other policy areas	General public, media, markets
Regularly	Extensive	Information on the course of meetings and discussions (presentation of the reasons behind the monetary policy decision, policy options.)	General public, media, markets
Regularly	Brief	Presentation of the voting behavior; explanation of dissenting positions	General public, media, markets

(*continued*)

Table A.1 (continued)

Instruments	Format	Channels	When
Further information on monetary policy and economic developments			
Reports (monthly bulletin, annual report, etc.)	Written	Website/ hard copy	
Publication of projections	Written	Website/ hard copy	
Publication of statistical data	Written	Website/ hard copy	As soon as confirmed
Publication of surveys	Written	Website/ hard copy	
Public hearings/ reports to the legislature	Verbal/written	Live reporting, print media, website/ hard copy	
Interviews	Verbal or written	TV, radio, and/or print media	
Speeches	Verbal	Direct interaction; TV, radio, and/ or reporting in the media (in most cases also website/ hard copy)	

Frequency	Detail	Content	Target group
Monthly/ quarterly/ annually	Extensive	Analysis of monetary policy issues and assessment of the current economic environment; special topics.	General public, media, markets
Quarterly/ biannually	Extensive		Analysts, ECB observers, interested members of the public
Regularly	Extensive	Money and banking statistics; balance of payments statistics; similar statistics	Analysts, ECB observers, interested members of the public
Regularly	Extensive		Analysts, interested members of the public
Regularly	Extensive	Explanation of monetary policy	Politicians, ECB observers, interested members of the public
Regularly	Brief or extensive	Key monetary policy issues (mandate, strategy, decisions); special topics; current problems regarding economic policy (fiscal policy, structural policy); topics of regional interest	National or regional public, media, markets
Regularly	Brief to extensive	Key monetary policy issues (mandate, strategy, decisions); special topics, current problems regarding economic policy (fiscal policy, structural policy); topics of regional interest	Specific

(continued)

Table A.1 (continued)

Instruments	Format	Channels	When
Briefings	Verbal	Central bank representatives meet with journalists in person	
Monetary policy research			
Research papers	Written	Publications in hard copy/on website	
Conferences	Verbal/written	Direct interaction and open dialogue, sometimes with media present, subsequently also website/hard copy	
Transfer of monetary policy knowledge			
Presentations/ visitor groups	Verbal	Direct interaction	
Information leaflets	Written	Website/hard copy	
Videos/video games	Audiovisual	Website/ presentation	
School competitions	Verbal and written	Direct interaction	

Source: Otmar Issing, "Communication, Transparency, Accountability: Monetary Policy in the Twenty-First Century," *Federal Reserve Bank of St. Louis Review* 87 (March/April 2005).

Frequency	Detail	Content	Target group
In most cases irregularly, in some cases also regularly	Extensive	Explanation of reactions, opinions, and central bank assessments to make monetary policy decisions more intelligible	Media representatives
Regularly	Specialized, sometimes highly complicated	Specialized fields; studies of monetary policy from general and academic points of view	Academics, interested members of the public
Regularly	Specialized, sometimes highly complicated	Specialized fields; studies of monetary policy from general and academic points of view	Academics, interested members of the public
Regularly	Brief to extensive	Range from a simple presentation to a detailed explanation of basic monetary policy issues	School pupils, students, CEOs, interested members of the public
Regularly	Brief to extensive	Range from a simple presentation to a detailed explanation of basic monetary policy issues	Children, teenagers, teachers, students, interested members of the public
Regularly	Brief to extensive	Range from a simple presentation to a detailed explanation of basic monetary policy issues	Children, teenagers, teachers, students, interested members of the public
Regularly	Extensive	Pedagogical introduction to the monetary policy decision-making process	Teenagers, teachers

References

Adam, Klaus. 2004. "Optimal Monetary Policy with Imperfect Common Knowledge." CEPR Discussion Paper 4594. London: Centre for Economic Policy Research, September.

Afonso, António, Michael G. Arghyrou, María Dolores Gadea, and Alexandros Kontonikas. 2018. "'Whatever It Takes' to Resolve the European Debt Crisis? Bond Pricing Regime Switches and Monetary Policy Effects." *Journal of International Money and Finance* 86(C): 1–30.

Barclays. 2013. "A Quantum Shift in Central Bank Communication." Barclays Economic Research, September 12.

Bernanke, Ben S. 2013. "Communication and Monetary Policy." Herbert Stein Memorial Lecture, Washington, D.C., November 19.

Bholat, David, Stephen Hansen, Pedro Santos, and Cheryl Schonhardt-Bailey. 2015. "Text Mining for Central Banks." CCBS Handbook 33. London: Bank of England, Centre for Central Banking Studies.

BIS (Bank for International Settlements). 2016. *86th Annual Report*. Basel: BIS.

Blinder, Alan S. 1998. *Central Banking in Theory and Practice*. Cambridge, MA: MIT Press.

Blinder, Alan S. 2000. "Central-Bank Credibility: Why Do We Care? How Do We Build It?" *American Economic Review* 90 (5): 1421–1431.

Blinder, Alan S. 2018. "Through a Crystal Ball Darkly: The Future of Monetary Policy Communication." *AEA Papers and Proceedings* 108 (May): 567–571.

Blinder, Alan S., Michael Ehrmann, Jakob de Haan, and David-Jan Jansen. 2017. "Necessity As the Mother of Invention: Monetary Policy after the Crisis." ECB Working Paper 2047. Frankfurt am Main: European Central Bank, April.

Blinder, Alan S., Michael Ehrmann, Marcel Fratzscher, Jakob de Haan, and David-Jan Jansen. 2008. "Central Bank Communication and Monetary Policy: A Survey of Theory and Evidence." *Journal of Economic Literature* 46 (4): 910–945.

Born, Benjamin, Michael Ehrmann, and Marcel Fratzscher. 2013. "Central Bank Communication on Financial Stability." *Economic Journal*, June. https://doi.org/10.1111/ecoj.12039.

Börsen-Zeitung. 2003. "Glossar der geldpolitischen Signalsprache der EZB," August 9.

Braun, Benjamin. 2017. "Two Sides of the Same Coin? Independence and Accountability of the European Central Bank." Transparency International EU. https://transparency.eu/wp-content/uploads/2017/03/TI-EU_ECB_Report_DIGITAL.pdf.

Brunner, Karl. 1981. "The Art of Central Banking." In *Geld, Banken und Versicherungen*, edited by Hermann Göppl and Rudolf Henn, vol. 1, 14–38. Königstein: Athenäum.

Buiter, Willem H. 1999. "Alice in Euroland." CEPR Policy Paper 1. London: Centre for Economic Policy Research, April.

Buiter, Willem H. 2014. "Central Banks: Powerful, Political and Unaccountable?" MPRA Paper 59477. Munich Personal RePEc Archive. https://mpra.ub.uni-muenchen.de/59477/1/MPRA_paper_59477.pdf.

Campbell, Jeffrey R., Charles L. Evans, Jonas D. M. Fisher, and Alejandro Justiniano. 2012. "Macroeconomic Effects of Federal Reserve Forward Guidance." *Brookings Papers on Economic Activity* 43, no. 1 (Spring).

Cicero, Marcus Tullius. (c66 BC) 1989. "De imperio Gnaei Pompeii." In *Werke in drei Bänden, Erster Band,* translated by Horst Dieter and Liselot Huchthausen, edited by Liselot Huchthausen, 210. Berlin: Aufbau.

Coenen, Günter, Michael Ehrmann, Gaetano Gaballo, Peter Hoffmann, Anton Nakov, Stefano Nardelli, Eric Persson, and Georg Srasser. 2017. "Communication of Monetary Policy in Unconventional Times." ECB Working Paper 2080. Frankfurt am Main: European Central Bank, June.

Coibion, Olivier, Yuriy Gorodnichenko, Saten Kumar, and Mathieu Pedemonte. 2018. "Inflation Expectations—a Policy Tool?" Paper presented at the ECB Forum on Central Banking, "Price and Wage-Setting in Advanced Economies," Sintra, Portugal, June 18–20.

Cole, Stephen J. 2018. "The Effectiveness of Central Bank Forward Guidance under Inflation and Price-Level Targeting." *Journal of Macroeconomics* 55(C): 146–151.

Constâncio, Vitor. 2018. "Completing the Odyssean Journey of the European Monetary Union." Remarks at the ECB colloquium, "The Future of Central Banking," Frankfurt am Main, May 16–17.

De Grauwe, Paul. 2013. "Central Bank Communication When Agents Experience Limitations." In *Central Bank Communication, Decision Making, and Governance,* edited by P. L. Sikklos and J. E. Sturm. Cambridge, MA: MIT Press.

De Larosière, Jacques, Leszek Balcerowicz, Otmar Issing, Rainer Masera, Callum McCarthy, Lars Nyberg, José Pérez, and Onno Ruding. 2009. *Report.* The High-Level Group on Financial Supervision in the EU. Brussels, February. http://ec.europa.eu/internal_market/finances/docs/de_larosiere_report_en.pdf.

Draghi, Mario. 2012. Speech at the Global Imvestor Conference in London, July 26.

Draghi, Mario. 2014. "Monetary Policy Communication in Turbulent Times." Paper presented at the Nederlandsche Bank conference, "200 Years: Central Banking in the Next Two Decades," Amsterdam, April 24.

Draghi, Mario. 2018. Press conference, Q&A, April 26.

Draghi, Mario. 2018. "Introductory Statement to the Press Conference," January 26.

Duisenberg, Willem. 2000. "Introductory Statement to the Press Conference." Frankfurt am Main: European Central Bank, April 14.

ECB (European Central Bank). 2002a. "The Accountability of the ECB." *Monthly Bulletin,* November, 45–58.

ECB. 2002b. "Transparency in the Monetary Policy of the ECB." *Monthly Bulletin,* November, 59–66.

ECB. 2014. "The ECB's Forward Guidance." *Monthly Bulletin*, April, 65–74.

ECB. 2018. "The Evolution of the ECB's Accountability Practices during the Crisis." *Economic Bulletin*, no. 5.

Economist, The. "How the Yuan Sets the Tone in Currency Markets," September 20, 2018.

Ehrmann, Michael, Sylvester Eijffinger, and Marcel Fratzscher. 2012. "The Role of Central Bank Transparency for Guiding Private Sector Forecasts." *Scandinavian Journal of Economics* 114 (3): 1018–1052.

Eusepi, Stefano, and Bruce Preston. 2018. "The Science of Monetary Policy: An Imperfect Knowledge Perspective." *Journal of Economic Literature* 56 (1): 3–59.

Fed. 2012. Federal Reserve issues FOMC statement, December 12.

Feroli, Michael, David Greenlaw, Peter Hooper, and Frederic S. Mishkin. 2017. "Language after Liftoff: Fed Communication away from the Zero Lower Bound." *Research in Economics* 71 (3): 452–490.

Finer, David Andrew. 2018. "What Insights Do Taxi Rides Offer into Federal Reserve Leakage?" Chicago: University of Chicago, Booth School of Business.

FOMC (Federal Open Market Committee). 2003. Press release, August 12.

FOMC. 2004. Minutes of the Federal Open Market Committee, January 27–28.

FOMC. 2011. Press release, August 9.

Friedman, Benjamin M. 2016. "Intellectual Origins of the Financial Crisis." Paper presented at the "Swiss National Bank Karl Brunner Centenary," September 23.

Goodhart, Charles A. E., and Lim Wen Bin. 2011. "Interest Rate Forecasts: A Pathology." *International Journal of Central Banking* 7, no. 2 (June): 135–171.

Goodhart, Charles, and Rosa Lastra. 2017. "Populism and Central Bank Independence." *Open Economies Review* 29, no. 1 (September 26): 49–68.

Greenfield, Charlotte, and Jane Wardell. 2018. "Hot Air Balloons: NZ Central Bank Chief Orr Tries to Demystify Monetary Policy." Reuters, May 10.

Haldane, Andrew G. 2017. "A Little More Conversation—a Little Less Action." Speech before the Federal Reserve Bank of San Francisco, March 31.

Hansen, Stephen, Michael McMahon, and Andrea Prat. 2018. "Transparency and Deliberation within the FOMC: A Computational Linguistic Approach." *Quarterly Journal of Economics* 133, no. 2 (May): 801–870.

Issing, Otmar. 1985. "Rationale Erwartungen—im Jahre 67 vor Christus." *Kyklos* 38, no. 1: 104–105.

Issing, Otmar. 1993. "Central Bank Independence and Monetary Stability." Institute of Economic Affairs Occasional Paper 89. London: Institute of Economic Affairs.

Issing, Otmar. 1999. "The Eurosystem: Transparent and Accountable, or Willem in Euroland." CEPR Policy Paper 2. London: Centre for Economic Policy Research, April.

Issing, Otmar. 2005. "Communication, Transparency, Accountability: Monetary Policy in the Twenty-First Century." *Federal Reserve Bank of St. Louis Review* 87, no. 2 (March/April): 65–83.

Issing, Otmar. 2008. *The Birth of the Euro.* Cambridge: Cambridge University Press.

Issing, Otmar. 2014. "Forward Guidance: A New Challenge for Central Banks." SAFE White Paper 16. Frankfurt am Main: Goethe University Frankfurt.

Issing, Otmar. 2017. "Central Banks—Are Their Reputations and Independence under Threat from Overburdening?" *International Finance* 20, no. 1: 92–99.

Issing, Otmar, Vitor Gaspar, Ignazio Angeloni, and Oreste Tristani. 2001. *Monetary Policy in the Euro Area.* Cambridge: Cambridge University Press.

Kahneman, Daniel. 2003. "Maps of Bounded Rationality: Psychology for Behavioral Economics." *American Economic Review* 93, no. 5 (December): 1449–1475.

King, Mervyn. 2002. "The Monetary Policy Committee: Five Years On." Speech before the Society of Business Economists, London, May 22.

King, Mervyn. 2004. "The Institutions of Monetary Policy." Robert T. Ely Lecture, 2004. Presented at the American Economic Association Annual Meeting, San Diego, January 4.

King, Mervyn. 2016a. *The End of Alchemy: Money, Banking, and the Future of the Global System.* New York: W. W. Norton.

King, Mervyn. 2016b. Interview. *Central Banking*, August 24. https://www.centralbanking.com/central-banks/financial-stability/2467506/mervyn-king-on-brexit-crisis-supervision-economic-rebalancing-and-reforming-the-imf.

Lucas, Robert E. Jr. 1976. "Econometric Policy Evaluation: A Critique." Carnegie-Rochester Conference Series on Public Policy 1. New York: Elsevier.

Lustenberger, Thomas, and Enzo Rossi. 2017a. "The Social Value of Information: A Test of Beauty and Non-Beauty Contest." SNB Working Paper 2017-17. Zurich: Swiss National Bank.

Lustenberger, Thomas, and Enzo Rossi. 2017b. "Does Central Bank Transparency and Communication Affect Financial and Macroeconomic Forecasts?" SNB Working Paper 2017-12. Zurich: Swiss National Bank.

Macmillan, H. 1931. *Report of the Committee on Finance and Industry.* London: HMSO.

Maio, Giovanni. 2017. "Der Schatten der Transparenz: Über die Entwertung der Chirurgie durch das Transparenzdiktat." *Der Chirurg* 88, no. 7 (July): 622–627.

Meyer, Laurence H. 2004. *A Term at the Fed: An Insider's View.* New York: HarperBusiness.

Mishkin, Frederic S. 2004. "Can Central Bank Transparency Go Too Far?" NBER Working Paper 10829. Cambridge, MA: National Bureau of Economic Research.

Moessner, Richhild, David-Jan Jansen, and Jakob de Haan. 2017. "Communication about Future Policy in Theory and Practice: A Survey." *Journal of Economic Survey* 31, no. 3: 678–711.

Morris, Stephen, and Shin Hyun Song. 2002. "Social Value of Public Information." *American Economic Review* 92, no. 5 (December): 1521–1534.

Morris, Stephen, and Shin Hyun Song. 2006. "Social Value of Public Information: Morris and Shin (2002) Is Actually Pro-transparency, Not Con: Reply." *American Economic Review* 96, no. 1 (March): 453–455.

Morris, Stephen, and Shin Hyun Song. 2018. "Central Bank Forward Guidance and the Signal Value of Market Prices." *AEA Papers and Proceedings* 108 (May): 572–577.

Muchlinski, Elke. 2014. "Why Do Markets React to Words?" *On the Horizon* 22 (4): 318–327.

Muchlinsky, Elke. 2011. *Central Banks and Coded Language: Risks and Benefits.* Basingstoke: Palgrave Macmillan.

Orphanides, Athanasios. 2011. "New Paradigms in Central Banking?" Central Bank of Cyprus Working Paper 2011-6. Cyprus: Central Bank of Cyprus.

Qvigstad, Jan F., and Tore Schei. 2018. "Criteria for 'Good' Justifications." Norges Bank Research, Working Paper 6/2018. Oslo: Norges Bank.

Samuelson, Paul A. 1994. "Panel Discussion, Goals, Guidelines and Constraints Facing Monetary Policymakers." Federal Reserve Bank of Boston, *Conference Series* 38.

Schmidt, Reiner. 2015. "Die entfesselte EZB." *Juristenzeitung* 70, no. 7 (April): 317–327, 3.

Shannon, C. E. 1948. "A Mathematical Theory of Communication." *Bell System Technical Journal* 27 (July, October): 379–423, 623–656.

Shin Hyun Song. 2017. "Can Central Banks Talk Too Much?" Speech at the ECB conference, "Communication Challenges for Policy Effectiveness, Accountability and Reputation," Frankfurt am Main, November 14.

Siekmann, Helmut. 2013. "Introduction, Article 119 and 130 AEUV." In *Kommentar zur Europäische Währungsunion,* edited by Helmut Siekmann. Tübingen: Mohr Siebeck.

Siekmann, Helmut, Vikrant Vig, and Volker Wieland, eds. 2015. "The ECB's Outright Monetary Transaction in the Courts." IMFS Interdisciplinary Studies in Monetary and Financial Stability 1. Frankfurt am

Main: Goethe University Frankfurt, Institute for Monetary and Financial Stability.

Sims, Christopher A. 2003. "Implications of Rational Inattention." *Journal of Monetary Economics* 50, no. 3 (April): 665–690.

Stein, Jeremy C. 2014. "Challenges for Monetary Policy Communication." Speech before the Money Marketeers of New York University, New York, May 6.

Sveriges Riksbank. 2010. Minutes of the Executive Board Meeting, September 1.

Svensson, Lars E. O. 2006. "Social Value of Public Information: Comment: Morris and Shin (2002) Is Actually Pro-transparency, Not Con." *American Economic Review* 96, no. 1 (March): 448–452.

Tucker, Paul. 2018. *Unelected Power.* Princeton, NJ: Princeton University Press.

Von Hayek, Friedrich A. (1962) 2007. "Regeln, Wahrnehmung und Verständlichkeit." In *Wirtschaftstheorie und Wissen*, edited by Viktor Vanberg. Tübingen: Mohr Siebeck.

Weidmann, Jens. 2018. "Notenbankkommunikation als geldpolitisches Instrument." Speech, Center for European Economic Research, Mannheim, May 2.

Wendschlag, Mikael. 2018. "Central Bankers in Twelve Countries between 1950 and 2000: The Making of a Global Elite." In *Financial Elites and European Banking: Historical Perspectives*, edited by Youssef Cassis and Giuseppe Telesca. Oxford: Oxford University Press.

Winkler, Bernhard. 2000. "Which Kind of Transparency? On the Need for Clarity in Monetary Policy-making." ECB Working Paper 26. Frankfurt am Main: European Central Bank, August.

Wittgenstein, Ludwig. 1922. *Tractatus Logico-Philosophicus.* London: Kegan Paul.

Woodford, Michael. 2005. "Central Bank Communication and Policy Effectiveness." In *The Greenspan Era: Lessons for the Future.* Kansas City, MO: Federal Reserve Bank of Kansas City.

Woodford, Michael. 2013. "Forward Guidance by Inflation-Targeting Central Banks." Paper presented at the conference "Two Decades of

Inflation Targeting: Main Lessons and Remaining Challenges," Sveriges Riksbank, Oslo, June 3.

Woodward, Bob. 2000. *Maestro: Greenspan's Fed and the American Boom.* New York: Simon and Schuster.

Yellen, Janet L. 2012. "Revolution and Evolution in Central Bank Communications." Speech at the Haas School of Business, University of California, Berkeley, November 13.

Index